Cultural Traditions in
Sri Lanka

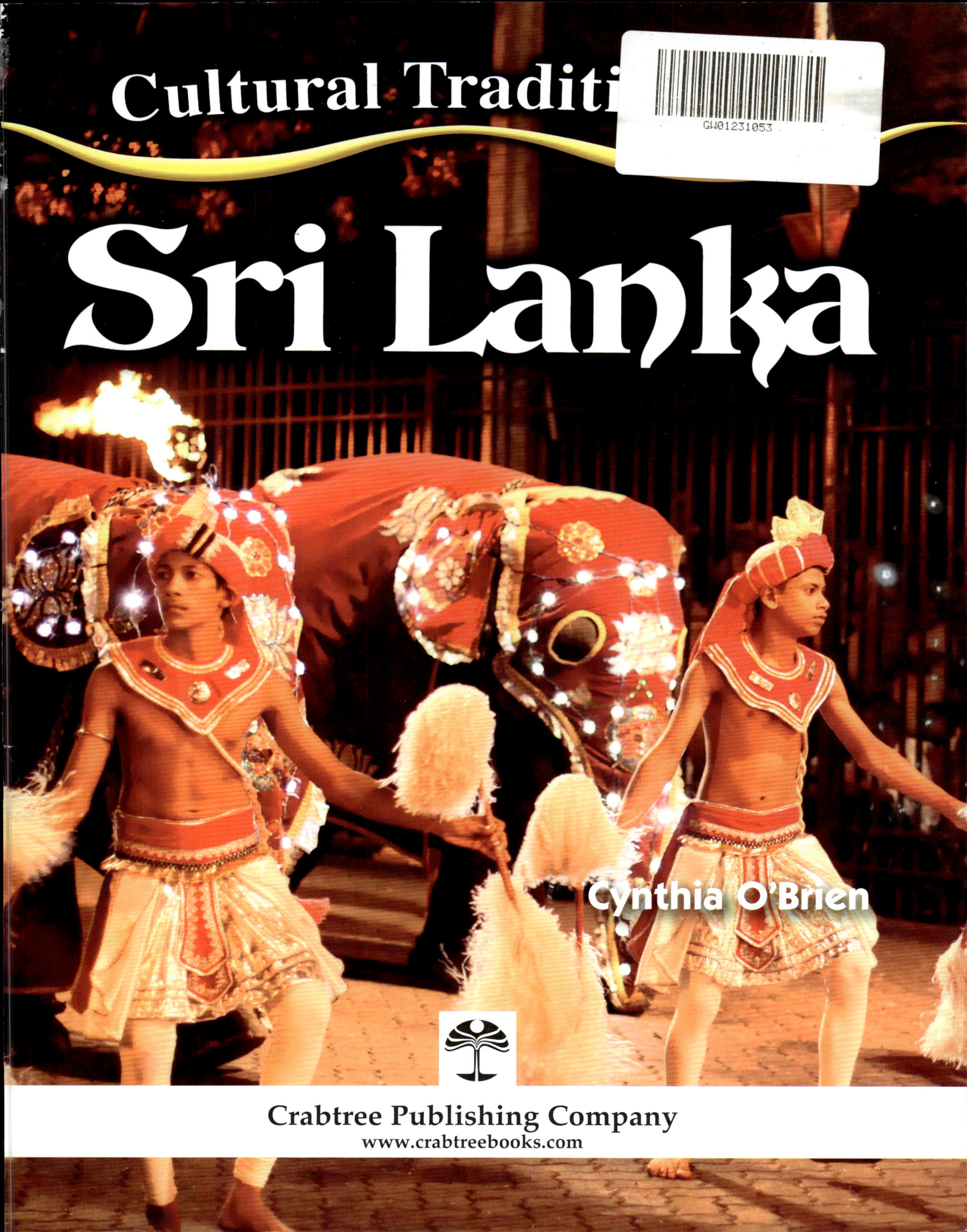

Cynthia O'Brien

Crabtree Publishing Company
www.crabtreebooks.com

Crabtree Publishing Company
www.crabtreebooks.com

Author: Cynthia O'Brien

Publishing plan research and development:
Reagan Miller

Editorial director: Kathy Middleton

Editor: Ellen Rodger

Proofreader: Wendy Scavuzzo

Photo research: Abigail Smith

Designer: Abigail Smith

Production coordinator and prepress technician:
Abigail Smith

Print coordinator: Margaret Amy Salter

Cover: elephants in a river (top, background); ocean fisher perched on pole (middle right); a traditional dancer (middle right); brightly painted traditional mask (bottom middle); tea (bottom left); lotus flower (bottom right); junglefowl (bottom right); tea plants growing on a plantation (bottom background)

Title page: Dancers at the Festival of the Tooth in Kandy, Sri Lanka

Photographs:
Alamy: Hemis, p9 (bkgd); Mohammed Abidally, p14 (bottom); F1online digitale Bildagentur GmbH; p15; Asia Images Group Pte Ltd, p21 (right); RM Asia, p23 (bottom); Mohammed Abidally, p27
Getty Images: Asanka Brendon Ratnayake, p8; LAKRUWAN WANNIARACHCHI, p28 (inset)
iStock: ertyo5, p11 (inset); Cameris, p21 (left); thefinalmiracle, p29 (bkgd); eyefocusaz, p31
Shutterstock: © Janaka Dharmasena, title page; © OlegD, p5 (inset); © Klemen Misic, p6; © Val Shevchenko, p7; © 123451, pp10–11 (bottom); © Natalia Davidovich, p17; © Dmitry Chulov, p19; © Thomas Wyness, p24 (left); © Saman527, p924 (bottom), p25; © Efimova Anna, p30
Wikimedia Commons: Brendan, p9 (right); lakpuratravels, p26; Amila Tennakoon, p28 (left); Jean-Pierre Dalbéra, front cover (dancer left)

All other images by Shutterstock

Library and Archives Canada Cataloguing in Publication

O'Brien, Cynthia (Cynthia J.), author
    Cultural traditions in Sri Lanka / Cynthia O'Brien.

(Cultural traditions in my world)
Includes index.
Issued in print and electronic formats.
ISBN 978-0-7787-8099-1 (hardcover).--
ISBN 978-0-7787-8107-3 (softcover).--
ISBN 978-1-4271-1954-4 (HTML)

    1. Holidays--Sri Lanka--Juvenile literature. 2. Festivals--Sri Lanka--Juvenile literature. 3. Sri Lanka--Social life and customs--Juvenile literature. I. Title. II. Series: Cultural traditions in my world

GT4876.2.A2O27 2017   j394.2695493   C2017-903530-4
                                                C2017-903531-2

Library of Congress Cataloging-in-Publication Data

Names: O'Brien, Cynthia (Cynthia J.), author.
Title: Cultural traditions in Sri Lanka / Cynthia O'Brien.
Description: New York, New York : Crabtree Publishing, 2018.
Series: Cultural traditions in my world | Includes index. |
    Audience: Age 5-8. | Audience: Grade K to 3.
Identifiers: LCCN 2017024408 (print) | LCCN 2017027911 (ebook) |
    ISBN 9781427119544 (Electronic HTML) |
    ISBN 9780778780991 (reinforced library binding) |
    ISBN 9780778781073 (pbk.)
Subjects: LCSH: Festivals--Sri Lanka--Juvenile literature. | Sri Lanka--Social life and customs--Juvenile literature.
Classification: LCC GT4876.2.A2 (ebook) | LCC GT4876.2.A2 O37 2018 (print) | DDC 394.2695493--dc23
LC record available at https://lccn.loc.gov/2017024408

Crabtree Publishing Company
www.crabtreebooks.com   1-800-387-7650

Printed in Canada/082017/EF20170629

Copyright © **2018 CRABTREE PUBLISHING COMPANY.** All rights reserved. No part of this publication may be reproduced, stored in a retrieval system or be transmitted in any form or by any means, electronic, mechanical, photocopying, recording, or otherwise, without the prior written permission of Crabtree Publishing Company. In Canada: We acknowledge the financial support of the Government of Canada through the Canada Book Fund for our publishing activities.

Published in Canada
Crabtree Publishing
616 Welland Ave.
St. Catharines, ON
L2M 5V6

Published in the United States
Crabtree Publishing
PMB 59051
350 Fifth Avenue, 59th Floor
New York, New York 10118

Published in the United Kingdom
Crabtree Publishing
Maritime House
Basin Road North, Hove
BN41 1WR

Published in Australia
Crabtree Publishing
3 Charles Street
Coburg North
VIC 3058

Contents

Welcome to Sri Lanka 4
Poya Days 6
Harvest Festival 8
Independence Day 10
Shiva Festival 12
New Year 14
May Days 16
Vesak 18
Poson Poya 20
Ramadan 22
Festival of the Tooth 24
Feast of the Assumption 26
Festival of Lights 28
Christmas 30
Glossary and Index 32

Welcome to Sri Lanka

The small island of Sri Lanka lies off the southern tip of India. Most Sri Lankans belong to two **ethnic** groups, the Sinhalese and the Tamils. They speak Sinhala and Tamil. The government also uses English. Most people in Sri Lanka are Sinhalese, and follow the **Buddhist** religion. Most Tamils follow the **Hindu** religion. Other Sri Lankans are **Muslim** or **Christian**.

Did You Know?
Sri Lanka has two nicknames because of its shape. It is called the "pearl of the Indian Ocean" and the "teardrop of India."

Sri Lankans have many celebrations and festivals. Many of the country's customs and traditions are more than 2,000 years old. The Buddhist religion influences many of Sri Lanka's celebrations. For these events, the country follows a Southern Buddhist **lunar calendar**. In lunar calendars, the dates of festivals can be different from year to year.

Colorful clothing, music, and dancing are often part of Sri Lanka's celebrations.

Poya Days

Siddhartha Gautama, or the Buddha, was born about 2,500 years ago. He was a spiritual, or religious, leader. Buddhism is a religion that follows his teachings. In Sri Lanka, Poya days are Buddhist celebrations that happen throughout the year. They fall on days that have a full moon, or about once a month. Most businesses close on Poya days.

This large statue of Buddha is in Colombo, Sri Lanka's capital city.

Did You Know? Selling or eating meat is not allowed on Poya days.

Sri Lankans play music and march in a Poya Day parade near the city of Unawatuba.

Poya days celebrate important events in the Buddha's life. Each one has its own name. For example, Poson Poya commemorates Buddha's arrival in Sri Lanka. In Sinhalese, "poy" comes from a word that means **fast** day. Buddhists spend the day fasting. Then they go to the **temple** to pray. The evening is filled with feasting, parades, and festivities.

Harvest Festival

In January, Tamil people in Sri Lanka celebrate Thai Pongal. It is a four-day harvest festival. Like Thanksgiving in North America, this is a time to be thankful for good crops, the Sun, and rain. During Thai Pongal, people clean and decorate their houses and wear new clothing.

Cattle are decorated with straw, flowers, and bells to celebrate Thai Pongal. Their horns may also be painted bright colors.

Thai Pongal is a Hindu celebration. It is a time for sharing. People play outdoor games together and set off fireworks at night. Hindu families share a great feast with each other and with non-Hindus. The delicious festival meal includes a sweet rice pudding called pongal.

Did You Know?
In Sri Lanka, there are many types of dances. Kulu Natuma is the Harvest Dance. Dancers act out the different stages of rice growing.

Sri Lankan Hindus pray at a temple in Colombo to give thanks for the harvest.

Independence Day

Great Britain ruled over Sri Lanka for 133 years. On February 4, 1948, Sri Lanka gained its independence. To be independent means to be able to rule itself. From February 4, 1948, the country has had its own government. Today, it is a national holiday.

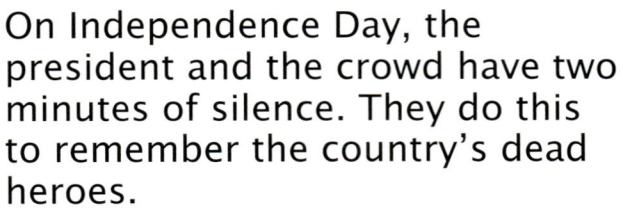

On Independence Day, the president and the crowd have two minutes of silence. They do this to remember the country's dead heroes.

On Independence Day, Sri Lankans celebrate with parades and traditional performances, such as dancing. There is a large **military** parade in Colombo, shown below. The president raises the Sri Lankan flag and gives a speech.

Dancers wearing traditional costumes perform on Independence Day.

Shiva Festival

Shiva is an important Hindu god. Maha Shivaratri means the Great Night of Shiva. This festival happens over a night and day during February. The dates change depending on the Hindu lunar calendar. In the morning of Maha Shivaratri, Hindus go to the temple. Bells ring to announce the day.

This statue of Shiva sits at the Koneswaram Hindu temple in eastern Sri Lanka.

Sri Lankan Tamils and other Hindus fast during Maha Shivaratri, and sing special chants and songs to honor Shiva. During the day, people also perform *sewas*. These are kind or **charitable** acts.

Did You Know?
People bring gifts to Shiva at the temple. Each one has a different meaning.

Lighting lamps represents knowledge.

Incense represents riches.

Fruit represents a long life.

New Year

Sri Lankan New Year happens in the middle of April. The festival celebrates the end of the harvest season. Sri Lankans clean their houses to represent a new beginning. They also wear new clothes. A special dish called *kiribath* is made with rice and coconut milk. Sweets such as cake and *kokis* are also served to family and friends.

Kokis are made from rice flour and coconut milk, and deep fried.

It is custom for women to light a fire and boil milk in the morning on New Year's Day. They make traditional foods with the milk.

Drumming is an important part of New Year celebrations. These men drum in a New Year parade in the town of Koggala.

Sinhalese families bless their children with oil. Tamil families give small gifts of money to children. The day is full of outdoor races and games, such as tug of war. The evening is time for music and dancing. Like many other countries around the world, the Sri Lankans welcome the New Year with spectacular fireworks.

May Days

May 1 is International Workers' Day. The government holds official celebrations in the capital. There and around the country, people go on marches. They speak out about problems in the country and ask for fair treatment for workers.

Did You Know?
Tea is one of Sri Lanka's main crops. Sri Lankans drink a lot of tea with warmed milk.

National Republic Day is May 22. On this day in 1972, Sri Lanka became a republic. In a republic, the people elect, or choose, government leaders. Sri Lankans also call this day National Heroes Day. Some of the day's celebrations honor Sri Lankan soldiers who have died.

The Sri Lankan flag is proudly woven on this day. On the first Republic Day, Sri Lankans flew their new flag for the first time.

Vesak

In May, Poya day is called Vesak. This holiday is sometimes referred to as "Buddha Day." It honors the birth and death of the Buddha. Sinhalese Sri Lankans make and paint large, wooden platforms especially for Vesak. These platforms are called *pandals*. They represent scenes from the Buddha's life.

Did You Know? Pandals are very large. They can be up to 70 feet (21 meters) tall. As many as 50,000 multicolored lightbulbs decorate a pandal.

During Vesak, **meditation** and good deeds are important. In many communities, food is shared at *dansalas*. Dansala means "open house." Dansalas offer free ice cream, rice, curry, and other treats. Temples are decorated with flowers. At night, the streets light up with pandals, lanterns, and oil lamps.

Sri Lankans light oil lamps at a temple in Colombo. The light is a symbol of Buddha's wisdom.

Poson Poya

Over 2,000 years ago, a prince from India brought Buddhism to Sri Lanka. He introduced the religion at Mihintale, a mountain peak near the city of Anuradhapura. Poson Poya celebrates this occasion in June. Today, Mihintale and Anuradhapura hold the largest celebration in the country.

Many Buddhists travel to visit the temple and statue of Buddha, shown below, at Mihintale.

Poson Poya is a time of great joy and religious devotion. People decorate their homes with lights and *kudu*. Kudu are special lanterns shaped like lotus flowers or stars. At night, parades go through the streets. These lively events include elephants, dancers, and drummers.

Did You Know? Buddhists climb 1,840 steps to reach the temple at Mihintale.

People bring flowers to the temples and light incense.

21

Ramadan

For one month every year, Muslims in Sri Lanka take part in Ramadan. This is a time of fasting and prayer. At the end of the month is the festival Eid al-Fitr. In Sri Lanka, Muslims observe Eid by waking before dawn to wash and put on new clothes. They then go to the **mosque** to pray. After prayers, people exchange hugs and blessings.

Did You Know?
Adam's Peak is important to Muslims and Buddhists. On the top of the hill is a large indent in the shape of a foot. Muslims claim it is the **Prophet** Adam's footprint. Buddhists claim that Buddha made the print.

Eid al-Fitr is a time for giving and celebrating. Children receive small gifts or money. Families and communities come together to share a great feast of traditional foods such as a rice dish called *biriyani*, shown to the left. People also give gifts of food to the poor.

Dates and other fruit are eaten to break the fast at Eid.

Many Muslims in Colombo gather to pray at a public park called Galle Face Green.

Festival of the Tooth

One of Sri Lanka's most dazzling celebrations takes place in Kandy. It is the Esala Perahera, or the Festival of the Tooth. The city's main temple holds Buddha's tooth. In ancient belief, the tooth has the power to bring rain. Every July or August, Buddhists and many others gather for ten days to honor the tooth.

Parades are held to honor the tooth. They feature dancers in colorful costumes.

Thousands of performers take part in the nightly parades. There are elephants, drumming, dancing, and singing. The elephants are dressed in colorful silk robes and lights, shown below.

Did You Know? Buddha's tooth is kept in the smallest of seven golden cases, one inside the other.

One of the elephants carries a **replica** of the tooth a special, golden cage.

Feast of the Assumption

Christians in Sri Lanka celebrate the Assumption on August 15. This is the day that Catholics believe Mary, the mother of Jesus, went to heaven. Sri Lankans hold this festival at Our Lady of Madhu **Shrine**. Every August, thousands of Catholics make the **pilgrimage** to the shrine.

The shrine is inside the Madhu Church, below. It is in the middle of the jungle in northwest Sri Lanka.

The shrine, above, is decorated for the Assumption. The statue of Mary is in the center, where the arrow points.

Did You Know?
No one knows who made the statue or how it came to Sri Lanka. According to legend, fishermen found the statue in a wooden box they pulled from the sea.

Decorations such as flags and flowers are put up at the shrine. People camp outside. On Assumption Day, an outdoor **mass** is held. Afterward, the statue of Mary is carried around the crowds. The statue is thought to have healing powers.

Festival of Lights

Deepavali, or Diwali, is a Hindu festival. The name Diwali comes from a word meaning "row of lights." In Sri Lanka, Tamils and other Hindus celebrate Diwali for five days in October or November. For the first four days, people clean and decorate their homes.

Small, clay oil lamps are placed in rows on doors, windows, and other places.

People make colorful *kolam*, a type of drawing, to celebrate Diwali.

On the last night of Diwali, there is a large light display inside and outdoors. People dress in their best clothing. They exchange gifts with their loved ones. A special gift is a sweet made from crystal sugar. People also share a feast of traditional foods. After dinner, there are fireworks to enjoy.

Did You Know?
The Diwali lights mean hope for the future and other good things.

Christmas

Christmas season in Sri Lanka begins with firecrackers on December 1. People decorate their homes and many have Christmas trees. There is a Sri Lankan Santa Claus. People call him Naththal Seeya. Just like Santa, Naththal Seeya brings gifts for children.

Christians in Sri Lanka go to church at midnight on Christmas Eve, or on Christmas morning.

Did You Know?
In 2016, Sri Lankans built the world's tallest Christmas tree in Colombo, shown here. It was as tall as 12 giraffes!

Families and friends gather on Christmas Day to exchange presents. Christmas food is a blend of European and Sri Lankan flavors. Many people serve turkey, curry, or spiced rice. Many Sri Lankans make a dessert called Love Cake. This treat contains cashew nuts and spices.

Glossary

Buddhist A person who believes in one God, whose teachings came from a messenger named Buddha

charitable To be generous and give gifts of food, money, or help

Christian Someone who follows the teachings of Jesus Christ, whom they believe to be the Son of God

ethnic Relating to a group with a common background or culture

fast To eat little or no food for a period of time

Hindu An ancient religion that began in India

incense A material that produces a pleasant smell when burned

lunar calendar A yearly chart based on the phases of the Moon

mass A Catholic religious ceremony

meditation Thinking deeply

military The army, navy, air force, or other armed forces of a country

mosque A Muslim place of worship

Muslim A person who practices Islam, a religion that follows one God through the teachings of the prophet Muhammad

pilgrimage A journey for a religious purpose

prophet A person believed to be a messenger from God

replica An exact copy of something

shrine A sacred place devoted to a saint or holy person

temple A building devoted to religious worship

Index

Buddha 6–7, 18–19, 22, 24–25
Buddhists 5, 6–7, 13, 20–21, 22, 24–25
Christians 5, 26–27, 30–31
elephants 20, 21, 25
fasting 7, 22, 23
foods 8, 9, 14, 19, 23, 29, 31

Hindus 5, 6, 9, 12, 13, 28
incense 13, 21
lunar calendar 4, 12
Muslims 5, 22–23
pandals 18, 19
parades 7, 10, 11, 20, 25
pilgrimages 22, 26
Poya days 6–7, 18–19, 20–21

processions 21, 24, 25
Sinhalese people 4, 5, 7, 14–15
soldiers, honoring 11, 17
tea industry 16
Tamils 4, 5, 8, 13, 14–15, 28
Workers' Day 16